Th

The Water Cat

Best wishes
Theresa
Tomlinson

Theresa Tomlinson

The Old Print Workshop

First published 1988 by Julia MacRae Books

This edition published in 2024 by The Old Print Workshop

A CIP catalogue record for this book is available from the British Library.

Tomlinson, Theresa
The Water Cat.
823'.914(F] PZ7
0-86203-367-5

ISBN 978-1-0369-0033-5

Book layout by Clare Brayshaw

Cover design and illustration by Rosie Maddocks

Prepared and printed by:

York Publishing Services Ltd
64 Hallfield Road
Layerthorpe
York YO31 7ZQ

Tel: 01904 431213

Website: www.yps-publishing.co.uk

For the children of

Carlin How and Skinningrove

Contents

CHAPTER ONE

Not bad at all

It was a small tabby cat, with dark green eyes, sitting on a rock in the middle of the stream. I turned to my brother Tom, who came plodging up through the water behind me.

"It's wet ... that cat," I said. "It's soaking wet and it's stuck on that rock."

Tom pushed past me, holding out his hand, smacking his lips.

"Watch it," I said. "It'll have you. It looks wild."

But the cat rubbed its wet chin gently against our Tom's fingers and began to purr. Tom giggled.

"Nah," he said. "It's lovely ... but it tickles."

I dug in my pocket and pulled out a clean hanky. "They hate being wet. I'm going to dry it ... poor thing."

I paddled over to the rock, glad I'd worn wellies, and picked it up carefully. It allowed me to carry it over the water to the bank. I sat down on a rock, near the opening to the small cave that we'd found, and started to rub it dry.

"It's got funny eyes," said Tom.

The cat purred gently on my lap, staring up at us.

"Yes ... they've lots of colours in them, green and grey and blue. It puts me in mind of the sea when it's rough."

I carried on rubbing, though we heard voices and splashing; I didn't want the cat to be scared away. A dark-haired lad with a curly-haired little girl came paddling up the stream. I thought they were going to go straight past, but the lad noticed the cat. He came over to us, grinning as though it was a joke.

"You'll not get that cat dry," he said. "I've tried that myself, but there's no chance. You'll not get that one dry."

It came into my mind to tell him not to be so daft and to mind his own business, but before I could get it said, I realised that my skirt was soaking wet. I lifted the cat up and water trickled down from its paws, as if I'd just then picked it up from the stream ... just that moment. I couldn't believe it. I had to stand up and put it down on the ground, so I could wring out my skirt.

I shook my head. "I don't know. I've rubbed it really dry, but it's still wet. It's soaked my handkerchief and my skirt."

"Aye," he said. "This cat's always wet. This un's a water cat."

The small girl came up and tickled the cat's head. "Water cat," she repeated.

He made me angry, that grinning boy. "Water cat?" I said. "There's no such thing as a water cat."

He just laughed again. "Well ... maybe there ain't meant to be, but this one is. It jumps about in the water ... this cat. It catches fish."

Ignorant, he is, I thought, but just then the cat rubbed its damp furry side against my legs, leaving a wet trail behind, and I couldn't really contradict him, though it seemed so daft.

The boy settled himself down on one of the rocks; he'd decided to stay, it seemed.

"I know you," he said. "You're Dolly Hindmarch's granddaughter, aren't you? Just moved into number ten ... end house, we call it."

I nodded. All the bad feelings came flooding back. Somehow the cat had made me forget for a moment, but the misery suddenly returned. It was only our third day here in Carlingrove, and I hated it.

"Where've you come from?" he asked.

"Sheffield," I muttered, staring at my muddy wellies.

Tom had gone off paddling with the little girl ... making friends as usual, and the cat splashing about, jumping at their ankles. I didn't want to be left to talk to this stupid boy. I didn't want to get to know anyone here.

"Big mucky place that, i'nt it ... Sheffield?"

I wanted to slap his face. "No more mucky than here. Mucky little place this is."

"Aye ... works is mucky," he agreed. "But you've got the moors, and you've got the river, and you've got the sea."

I pulled a face. Moors and sea meant nothing to me. I wanted my old school and friends, and my old house that I'd felt so used to. My mam was always going on about moors and sea ... I was sick of hearing it.

"It'll take you a while to get used," he said. "'Specially living in end house. You know what they say, do you?

End house, end house,

Drive you round, the bend house."

Suddenly I couldn't help but laugh. "They're flaming well right an' all."

I thought the house was a right dump. I'd never seen anything like it before. It was a small house, next to the great gates of the steelworks. As if that wasn't bad enough, an overhead cable system brought buckets of iron ore up the hill from the mine in the valley. The buckets were tipped into a chute, just at the side of end house, so that a huge clattering and crashing went on all day, and a cloud of gingery red dust rose from the chute, and sprinkled itself gently over the backyard, every time a bucket was tipped. The backs of the houses looked out onto an ancient slag heap. I couldn't believe Mam wanted to come and live here. Even my dad had come back laughing and sighing from his first shift in the blast furnace.

"It's a rum place, Ivy," he'd said to Mam. "They've been telling me some tales. Fastest racing pigeons in England they've got here, so they claim. All sorts of funny goings-on I've been hearing about. They're even on about a merman. Did you ever? They say a merman lived here. You'd think they believed it, too."

"Oh the merman," said Mam. "Of course they believe it ... it's true."

Dad, he just roared with laughter, but I thought they were all crackers, and our mam as cracked as any.

"We've only moved into end house while we look for another," I told the boy.

"That's what Frank Wetherall used to say. He lived there before you. He said that, all the time, but they were there ten years before they moved. Mind you, he said that he got so he didn't notice the tipping ... only bothered him when it stopped. Gives you a shock when it stops, that's what he said. You'll get used to it, too. Will you be going 'up the valley' then?"

I stared at him, not understanding, thinking, we live up the valley already don't we?

"Up the valley," he said, "Carlingrove School."

I saw what he meant then. "Oh yes – 'up the valley'. I've not passed the exam though, so I'll be off to the Sec. Mod. come September."

"Me an' all. A right year it is, first the eleven – plus, now the coronation. Coronation'll be grand though; we're planning a good do for that."

I sighed. "There'll be some good do's in Sheffield, though."

We sat there awkward and silent for a while. I watched the little kids playing with the cat and I got an idea that made me feel a lot better.

"I'm going to take that cat home."

The boy shook his head.

"I am. Mam said we could have a cat when we came to Carlingrove. It's a better place for keeping a cat than Sheffield. She said that, she promised."

"It's not your mam," he said. "It's the cat."

"It looks like a stray," I insisted. "What's it doing down here? It needs a proper home. It needs looking after."

"Nay, you'll not get that cat back to the village ... it's a wild cat, a water cat, and there's the old fella."

"Old fella?"

"I don't really know ... but sometimes there's an old man down here. Tramp or summat. The kids say it's his cat."

I wasn't going to take any notice of that. The thought of taking the cat home cheered me up; nothing the boy said was going to stop me.

"Well, where is he?" I said. "He's not taking care of it; needs looking after properly."

I splashed through the water to the younger ones, and the cat.

"We're taking it home. I need something to tie round its neck, to lead it like."

Tom's face lit up. I could see he wanted it, too.

"Give us your braces," I said.

"No! Not me braces," he yelled, and grabbed

at his middle. "They're new, and me trousers fall down without them."

"Do you want the cat or not?" I said.

Tom sighed and nodded.

"Away back home our Mary," said the boy. "Mam'll have finished with washing by now."

A few minutes later we were all set to climb back up the hill to the village. I'd fastened one strap of Tom's braces round the cat's neck, and I held the other end like a lead. Tom was hitching at his trousers, but he kept cheerful, talking to the other lad. I could see he didn't want to appear grumpy. Little Mary ran ahead, then back to stroke the cat, then off ahead again.

We walked back beside the stream, heading towards the old stone bridge, following the path that led beneath the overhead cable system, then up through a field of goats, up to our houses.

The cat didn't seem to mind being led along like a dog – well, not at first, but when we got close to the bridge it began to pull back. I thought it must be getting tired, so I bent to pick it up. I was surprised how heavy it was; it hadn't felt so heavy when I'd picked it up before.

"Oof ... I can't carry you all the way," I said.

"You'll not get it back," our know-it-all friend said once again.

I put it down and tried to pull it along, but it lay down by my feet with a pitiful cry.

"Here ... that's too tight ont's neck," the boy said sharply.

"No," I said, though I was really puzzled. I put my hand beneath the knot. "Look, there's plenty of room." I let go of the braces and stroked the cat gently. "What's a matter puss? What's up then?"

It stared up at us real mournful. I panicked a bit. It's never going to die, I thought. I felt terrible. Then it rolled over and painfully it managed a few paces back upstream. It crawled further along, back where we'd come from, then at last it seemed to have perked up. We just stared: the further away it went, the better it looked, until at last it was running fine, Tom's braces still trailing behind it. We never moved, just watched as though we were spellbound. It was only when it disappeared that Tom let out a great cry.

"Now look what you've done with me braces!"

I knew it wouldn't do any good to go chasing after the cat just then, and we should've been getting home ... Mam'd be worrying. I hated having to give in though, and walk back up the hill with that lad. At least he kept quiet, and never said 'told you so'.

It was only when we got to the top of the bank, and climbed out onto the tarmac road near our house, that he spoke.

"Do you like pigeons?"

"They're okay I suppose."

"I like 'em," said Tom.

"I'll take you to our pigeon loft if you like ... could go tomorrow."

"Yes," said Tom. I had a feeling that our Tom would say 'yes' to anything this lad suggested.

"Me name's Fred."

"I'm Tom. She's Jane."

"I know – Mam told me. My mam used to go to school with yours. In the same class they were. Well, see you then. Away home our Mary."

He went off down the street holding Mary's hand. I stared after him. He wasn't bad really. He wasn't bad at all and I'd been a bit rude to him.

CHAPTER TWO

Dreaming

I couldn't get to sleep that night, I couldn't settle. My old chest of drawers and wardrobe made scary shapes in the strange bedroom. I got out of bed and wandered over to the window, staring out over the dark steelworks. You could tell the night shift were at work from the distant clanging and sudden flare of sparks under the dim yellow lights. The sky on the far side was lit with a rosy glow, but it wasn't the dawn, just the white-hot slag, slowly turning golden-red, on the tip beyond the village. Mam had shown me that the night before.

I'd never get used to this place, I thought. The only thing that raised a spark of interest was that cat. Now that was a real mystery, that was, and I really wanted to find it again. The more I thought about the cat, the more grumpy I got, until at last

I realised that there really was something wrong. I was cold, standing there in my nightie, with bare feet on bare floorboards, and I was hungry. I opened my bedroom door and jumped at the sight of a white figure standing at the top of our stairs.

"What's up then? Can't you sleep love?" It was Mam.

"I'm hungry Mam. I shall have to go and get myself summat."

"Eeh lass," she said. "Well ... there's some of that apple pie left, though you and our Tom between you put quite a bit away at tea-time."

I frowned. She was right. We had eaten quite a lot. I couldn't be hungry after that and, as soon as I thought about it, the feeling of hunger vanished. Went just as quick as it had come.

"Away back to bed love ... you're just unsettled. Back to your bed, and get some sleep. You'll be right as rain in the morning."

I let her take me back and tuck me in, like I was a bairn again, and I must have slept straight off, for the next thing I remembered was the clattering sounds as the buckets began tipping, and the tramp, tramp of boots as the morning shift came marching past and flooding in through the works gates, just below my window.

I got our Tom out of the house early, hoping to be off before Fred came looking for us. "I want to go down to the sea," I said.

I wasn't really bothered about the sea. I didn't think that a scrubby little place like Carlingrove could have a decent bit of beach anyway, but I didn't want to have to go off with Fred, to see his stupid pigeons. Mam'd said that Tom had to stay with me, just while we got to know our way round. She was worried he'd get lost if he went out on his own, and he would too; he was always getting lost. I'd tried to hurry him up, but he made as much trouble as he could. He'd lost one of his shoes, then when he'd found it, he snapped a shoe-lace. He sat down on the pavement outside our front gate, and wouldn't move. Then I saw him smiling all sly ... he'd seen Fred coming up the street towards us.

"Are we off to see our pigeons then?" said Fred.

It was then that I'd started on about the sea, but Fred had an answer for everything.

"Why ... we can come back round by the shore," he said, and swung himself over the gate that opened onto the goats' field path.

Tom set off after him, pleased as punch.

"Do you eat your pigeons, Fred?"

"Nah ... we just race 'em."

I followed, slowly trailing behind. There didn't seem to be anything else to do.

The pigeon huts were on the far side of the valley. We had to follow the same path that we'd taken before, but this time we crossed the stone bridge. Some strongly built sheds on the far side of the river covered the opening to the mines. Drift mines, Dad had called them, with tunnels, stretching far into the hillside. It was from those sheds that the buckets of iron ore started on their journey up the hill, past end house. Full, heavy buckets came steadily up the steep slope, while empty buckets went back to the mine, creaking and swinging about, all the way down the hillside, high above our heads.

I followed the boys over the bridge, still trailing behind them. I could just catch glimpses of the rolling grey sea in the distance. My stomach lurched as I leaned over the side of the bridge and that strange hungry, faint feeling that I'd had in the night came back. I grabbed onto the stone slabs to steady myself.

"Are you all right?" Fred had come back. He was standing beside me, frowning. "You don't look so good."

"I'm fine," I told him and walked on to the other side of the bridge. The feeling had gone and

I did feel fine, but I stopped for a moment to stare upriver, towards the cave, where we'd found the cat.

"Looking for that cat are you?" said Fred. "You never see it down here."

I certainly couldn't see any sign of it.

"It'll be there, near the cave .... always is."

"Come on you two," Tom yelled. "I want to see the pigeons."

Fred ran ahead and unlocked the door of the pigeon hut. He disappeared inside, then we heard thud ... thud ... thud, as little trapdoors flopped open, and out of them rushed the pigeons. The space around the hut was filled with beating wings. I stopped, scared to go any closer. Beaks, wings, claws going mad in all directions, then up they went, up into the sky with a great whoosh, and turned into fat dots that speckled the sky. Me and Tom stared.

"Grand sight, aren't they?" Fred stepped out from the doorway.

"There's hundreds of 'em," said Tom.

"There's fifty ... about fifty. Away in then — you can see the squeakers."

I wasn't sure about it at all, but I ducked my head and followed Tom in. You could stand straight once inside. It smelt of warm sour bread. Opposite the open flaps were little boxes … some with pigeons' heads sticking out.

"These've got babies ... chicks," said Fred. He lifted one of the birds and peered beneath, then replaced it with a firm stroke. "Thought so ... just hatched ... best leave them be. You can look at these, they're a bit bigger. Squabs these are, I call them squeakers."

He reached inside a box and brought out a tiny pigeon.

"Hold out," he said, and before I'd thought whether I wanted to or not, I'd a shaky little pigeon, covered in yellow down with tufts of sprouting blue, wobbling about in my hands.

"Oh, me too, me too," begged Tom.

It's funny how holding a small warm creature in your hands can make you feel soft inside ... soft and somehow better. I stared down at the ugly little thing, as Fred reached another down for Tom. It squeaked continually; squeaker seemed a good name. Its head was too big for its body and I couldn't help but smile at it.

"Best put 'em back before the big birds come," Fred said.

I handed my squeaker back reluctantly.

We heard a fluttering outside, and a large sleek bird landed on one of the flaps, then perched on Fred's shoulder.

"He's my favourite. Bluey I call him. He's always first back. Likes a bit of fuss, he does." Fred put his hand down into a sack and brought out a handful of small brown peas. Bluey gobbled them.

"Ugh, they look horrible," said Tom.

"He thinks they're a treat, and they're not bad with salt and vinegar."

We both stared at him. "You don't mean for people?" I said.

"Just for Carlin Sunday. Hasn't yer mam said owt about Carlin Sunday?"

"What's Carlin Sunday?" said Tom.

"Well, every year, on a certain Sunday – it was just before you came – we eat carlins, these little pigeon peas."

They *are* all crackers round here, I thought. "Whatever do you do that for?" I asked.

"It's a tradition. It's an old story ... there was a famine, see. Everyone was starving ... really bad it was. But just in time, a ship was wrecked off the bay. Well, the ship was full of carlins, see! The people ate the carlins and that saved their lives. They managed through to the next harvest and the fishing picked up. Now we eat carlins just once a year, to remember it all."

"Can I do it?" Tom asked.

"Aye ... but you'll have to wait till the proper day again. My mam, she soaks 'em and fries 'em in bacon fat, and then we sprinkle vinegar on them. You ask your mam – she'll know all about it, from when she were little."

Well, I've heard some stories, I thought.

We walked back down the hill, heading straight towards the sea. I could see the old stone bridge in the distance, behind us and I saw someone standing on it, looking out to sea ... standing just where I'd stood. I thought it must be an old woman because she was wearing a shawl over her head. Only an old woman would wear that, I thought.

We reached another more modern bridge, close to the sea front. It was all just what I'd imagined; a small shingle beach, with rusty old pipes lying around and an old broken down jetty, sticking out into the sea, below the steelworks road.

"Not much to see, is there?" I said.

"Oh, you've not seen Cattersty sands yet." Fred insisted. "The sands is best bit, way beyond the jetty."

So I followed him, along a path that led to the jetty, wondering why I was bothering, when suddenly, between some rusty disused trucks, I glimpsed golden sands. I caught my breath. Wide, rolling sands they were, wide and wild ... not a pretty seaside beach, but more like a desert with tough, reedy grass growing at the edges. I looked up at the rusty, corrugated iron sheds of the works on the hill above us, then back to the beautiful beach. They couldn't be side by side like that ... but there they were.

Fred and Tom went running ahead. I stopped to take off my shoes and socks, then I followed them. Tom rushed into the sea, and soaked his plimsolls before he'd' thought to take them off. He jumped over waves, screaming and yelling. I slowly climbed over the sand-hills, letting my toes sink into soft, warm sand. I flopped down and lay on my stomach and listened to the swish and lap of the waves. A great feeling of contentment washed over me, as I watched a young girl paddling at the edge of the sea. She'd a long skirt caught up round her waist. That's the second person I've seen today in old-fashioned clothes. There was a little animal jumping about near the girl, perhaps a dog ... no it's too small and it's got a long tail. I was so sleepy I couldn't be bothered to find out ... not another water cat, I thought.

"Come on Jane. You've been lying there for ages," said Tom.

I realised I'd fallen asleep. I pulled myself up. The girl in the long skirt had gone.

"Where is she?" I said. "Where's that little lass with a dog?"

"Hey?" said Fred. "There's no other lass here, but you. You've been asleep, you've been dreaming."

"Dreaming? Maybe I have ... for it wasn't a dog, it was another water cat."

"You have been dreaming" said Fred. "There's only the one and I've never seen it here."

"I can't get that funny cat out of my mind," I said. "I want to see if it's all right. I'm going to look for it tomorrow."

"Shall I come?" asked Fred.

"Can if you like," I nodded. "But we'd best be getting home now."

"I hope it's still got me braces," said Tom.

CHAPTER THREE

The worst thing you could say

I woke up in the middle of the night again, feeling hungry. I crept downstairs and opened the pantry door. There was a fine big chocolate cake that Mam'd made for our tea. Half of it was left. I cut myself a good slice, but then I remembered that I'd eaten quite a lot for my tea. The hunger faded away as before and I realised that my feet throbbed with cold, on the stone tiled floor. I put the cake back and turned to go At last I climbed back to bed, shivering with cold and feeling very puzzled about it all.

We set off the next morning, heading down to the cave to find the cat. Tom was being a nuisance. He wanted to go to the beach again.

I could hear Fred in the distance. "Away now lad ... we're off to find that cat again."

I marched on ahead. I was sick of having to trail my stupid brother around, and I was tired out, too. I hadn't had a good night's sleep at all, and I'd lain awake thinking about the story Fred had told us about the famine, and thinking how nasty it'd be if there wasn't a pantry full of Mam's good food downstairs. I'd just got myself off to sleep, but then the tipping had started. There was no wonder I felt as cross as I did.

I passed the old bridge, remembering how sick I'd felt last time when I stood on it, and set off, fast up the valley, away from the sea.

I spied the cat, long before I got to the cave, though I couldn't see it clear, just the silhouette, perched up on a high rock. It seemed to be staring at me ... or maybe past me, down to the sea. There was something about it that made me stop. It looked lonely, stretching its neck, straining to see as far down the valley as it could.

I moved forward again, slipping on the rocks, making a noise. I think it saw me then; for it jumped down and disappeared.

Damn it, I thought. I bet I've scared it now.

I got to the cave ... but there was no sign of the cat. I thought it might be hiding inside, so I went in after it ... a bit cautious. I looked carefully into the shadowy corners, but the cat wasn't there. Then I got a funny feeling that someone was watching me, that feeling when your back goes all shivery. I turned round slowly, but there was no one outside. I was just going to walk out into the sun when my stomach gave a horrid lurch. I was being watched. To the side of the cave was a small opening; it let a bit of light in. Through that small hole I thought I saw a pair of eyes. They stared straight at me, then flashed round the inside of the cave ... then vanished.

I daren't move. That wasn't the cat, I thought.

I heard footsteps then, and cheerful whistling. Fred, I thought, surprisingly relieved to know that he was there.

"Fred?" I called. "Fred ... is that you?"

Fred stepped inside the cave.

"Is anyone out there?" I whispered.

"No," he said, and he frowned as though he thought I was daft. "No ... what's up then?"

"There was someone there and they were watching me."

I felt a bit stupid, but I knew I hadn't imagined it. Fred looked a bit thoughtful then and he didn't say I was barmy, like he could have done.

"Well — could it have been the old fella?"

I remembered what he'd told me about the cat perhaps having an owner.

I shook my head. "They were right funny eyes."

"Aye," said Fred. "He's a right funny old fella – if it's him."

"It scared me a bit," I admitted. "It gave me a turn, but I think I scared him, too. They looked frightened, those eyes."

Tom came splashing through the water. I could see from his face that he'd still got the sulks, but I'd no patience left. I pushed past as he came into the cave.

"Give me some air," I said.

I felt better outside. I leant back against the rock, taking a deep breath and turning my face to the sun. Then my back stiffened, and I froze. On the far side of the beck was an old man ... just like Fred had said … a strange old fella. He had a beard and long silvery hair that streamed out behind and floated around his shoulders onto peculiar clothing that seemed to be made of a shiny green-brown stuff. He wasn't looking at me, but stared down the valley towards the sea. He stared with such sadness and longing that I felt rude, just being there, watching him.

Our Tom came out of the cave, kicking a rock in front of him. The old fella turned at the noise and looked straight at me. I knew at once, his eyes ... it had been his eyes spying on me inside the cave.

"What's up?" said Tom.

"Shut up," I hissed at him. Then when I looked back, the old man had gone.

Ignoring our Tom, I whispered to Fred. "He's here ... the old fella."

"Where?" said Fred, looking round.

"Who … who's here?" said Tom, looking from me to Fred.

Neither of us knew what to say and Tom was upset.

"You've got secrets," he cried. "You've got secrets from me. I don't care ... I want to go to the beach, anyway. I'm going ... I'm going on me own, and I'll tell me mam of you."

He turned and ran off, down the path beside the beck.

Fred looked worried. "I'll get after him."

"No," I said. "Leave him be. He's nothing but a nuisance and I want to find the old fella. I'm going to ask him about the cat. He's over behind those rocks. Come on, come with me."

I didn't want him to leave me alone with that weird old man. I waded through the water, trying not to slip on the pebbles and headed towards the rocks on the far side, near to the place where I'd seen him. Fred followed.

"What's that?"

Fred stopped and we both listened. The sound came again and I could see from Fred's face that he heard it, too. A bubbling, humming sound ... hard to hear over the rushing of the beck, but it rose strong then soft in a swishing rhythm that put me in mind of the rush of waves at the edge of the sea.

I moved forward again, trying to follow the sound, and clambered over a rock. Then I saw him, the old man. He was sitting on a rock, bending over to swish his hands in the water. His shiny long coat trailed right into the beck, getting soaked. He had his back to us and he was so busy that he didn't notice us coming up quietly beside him. His hands moved gently in time with the humming. He swished them through the water, to make a miniature wave swirl up onto the gravelly shore of the beck.

His hands paused; he knew that we were there. Slowly he pulled himself up, looking with horror at his hands.

"Alas, fingers where there should be paws; my power fails."

I turned to Fred, who just stared; his mouth dropped open. I saw that he'd be no help.

I cleared my throat. "Er um ... nice afternoon, isn't it?"

The old man looked bewildered, but then he seemed to find his courage and decide that perhaps we weren't so bad. He pulled himself up tall, and bowed his head in a very dignified way.

"Greetings fair maid and charming youth. You have caught me all adrift, but never fear, you are welcome visitors to my poor abode."

That took me by surprise; he might be mad, but he was certainly trying to be polite. I remembered hearing about some duke's son, who'd run away to live as a tramp. I felt then that it was us who were being rude, just gawping like that, and so I did the only thing I could think of. I dropped a curtsey. I'd learnt to do it in our dancing class – 'step to the side, put your foot behind – and curtsey'. It was the right thing to do too, because when I looked up he was smiling and nodding his head.

"My name," he said, "is Catterstyn."

There was an awkward silence, then I realised that we should tell him ours.

"I'm Jane ... Jane Johnston, and this is Fred ... er ..."

"Oh ... Fred ... Fred Metcalfe. " Fred was acting real stupid, frowning like mad.

"Were there not three of you?" Catterstyn asked.

"Three? Oh yes ... there was my brother Tom. He ... he went to the beach."

Again the uneasy silence.

At last he said, "I am not used to company, not for many years."

I remembered then what I'd really come for. "Please sir, the little water cat, does it belong to you?"

"Ah yes," he said. "The cat. Yes ... yes it does belong to me."

Fred started nudging me. "Ask him if it's here," he whispered.

I gave him a dirty look. I couldn't see why he was acting so stupid, but I asked about the cat.

"Alas ... he's not here today ... please visit him another day," said Catterstyn.

"Do you live here then?" I asked.

"Yes. Many years I have lived here. I have made this rough cave my home."

"Ah ha," said Fred, seeming to wake up at last. "You must be a great age then ... sir?"

Catterstyn smiled proudly. "A great age indeed."

He was that proud you could see. I thought I'd ask more. "How old?" I said. "Not as old as my gran, I bet?"

"What?" The smile fell like water from his face and I could see that he was suddenly furious, but I couldn't see why.

Fred grabbed my arm. "No, you've done wrong."

The old man was shaking, shaking with anger, his fists clenched, his hair quivering.

"Go," he ordered.

Fred pulled at me.

"No," I shouted. "What have I done? I've done nowt wrong."

Fred wouldn't take any notice, just pulled me away, past rocks, down the path, back towards the village.

"Get off," I yelled. "Why should I go?"

I slapped him with my free hand and thumped on his back till my hand throbbed, but he wouldn't let go, and he wouldn't stop.

"Just come away. I'll tell you – I will, but leave him be for now."

I looked back and saw the cat high up on a rock, its back arched black against the sun. I shrieked and pointed at it. At last Fred stopped.

"Aye, the cat. He would be there now. Come away and I'll tell you what's up."

Fred wouldn't stop till we reached the goats' field, but then he flopped down in the long grass at the bottom, getting his breath.

"Whew ... you've got a right fist you have. I'll say that for you."

I was still blazing angry. "Well?" I said. "You tell me what's up or you'll get it again."

He sat up and glared at me. "Don't you know anything about mermen?"

"What? You're crackers like the rest. There's no such thing as mermen." I spat it out.

"That's what you said about the water cat, at first."

He'd got me there. I stared at him. My brain couldn't take it in.

"I know it sounds crazy," he said. "I know it does, but there's a lot of things that all add up."

"What? What things?" Nothing seemed to make any sense to me.

"Well... he's very old and there's the cat."

"The cat ... so what?"

"That's what I mean. Don't you know that mermen are supposed to be shape-changers – especially where cats are concerned?"

"What?" I said. Some vague idea of what he meant began to come through. "You don't mean...?"

"Yes. You never see the old man and the cat together. Then there's his age. Don't you know about a merman's age?"

"What about it?"

"Your mam would know, but I don't suppose she'd think to tell you. They say that if you can discover the true age of a merman, then you'll have him in your power. He'll be your slave. So you see..."

"Oh, no." Understanding came to me at last and I heaved a huge, regretful sigh. "He'd be angry, real angry... and he was."

"It's the worst thing you could have said." Fred was merciless.

I shook my head. "I can't believe it. You're saying that the old man is really a merman, and sometimes he turns himself into a cat ... and to cap it all, I've offended him?"

"Well it does all fit in."

Am I going mad like the rest of them? I wondered.

"If it's true, it's fantastic," I said, "but now I've messed it all up."

"Well… he was so angry," said Fred. "I thought we'd best get out of the way quick. I didn't know what he would do. I told you mermen are shape-changers. It's not just cats that they change into."

"But he seemed fine at first. He was polite, he was kind."

"Yes he was. If we give him a chance to calm down, perhaps we could go back later and explain. We could tell him that you didn't understand. You could say you're sorry. Perhaps we could get back to being friendly again."

I am going mad, I thought. I felt silly and scared at the thought of going back to apologise, but what kept coming into my mind was the green changing eyes of the cat, and the way it had butted its soft head against my hand, and purred when I'd tried to get it dry.

"All right," I agreed. "We'll try."

"Don't look now," said Fred, "but we're being watched."

My stomach tightened.

"No ... no," Fred laughed. "It's Tom. He's spying on us from behind the bushes."

"Oh, him." I was glad it was only him.

"We should tell him," said Fred. "He thinks we're being mean."

"All right. You tell him. He takes notice of you."

Tom's eyes grew wider and wider as Fred told him what had happened.

"Wow ... that cat," he said.

It was funny how Tom believed it; he believed it straightaway. I couldn't believe it just like that. Perhaps if I'd been younger like Tom, I might have.

"And did he have a real fish's tail?" he asked. Fred and I looked at each other.

"He wore something long ... a cloak ... sort of shining," I said.

Tom was disappointed. "Didn't you notice?" he said, disgusted with us. "Of course he'd be a real merman if he had a fish's tail."

CHAPTER FOUR

Sledging with no snow

I stood on the doorstep of Fred's house, my hand raised to the knocker. I didn't really want to do it. I didn't really want to go calling for a lad, but there was only Fred that I'd got to know in the village and I daren't go looking for that strange Catterstyn with just our Tom.

"Go on then. What you waiting for?" Tom kicked at the fence with impatience.

I gritted my teeth and knocked, then stood back. I saw I'd made two dirty footprints on the freshly whitened step.

"Eh ... you mucky thing," said Tom.

It was Fred's mam who answered. "Away in love. You'll be Ivy Johnston's lass. Come on in, little 'un an all."

She was real friendly and never noticed the step. Once we were in there I couldn't think what to say, but I needn't have worried, for Fred's mam did the talking. She made us sit down and have lemonade and cakes and shouted Fred in from the backyard. She asked me about Sheffield and then started on about my mam and her being at school together. She fetched out her old photograph album. Really it was interesting and I'd have liked to listen, but I'd got that cat on my mind and I was worrying about trying to say sorry to Catterstyn. If we were really going to do it, I wanted to get it done.

"Can we get off, down to the beck?" I hissed at Fred while his mother's back was turned.

"Well, you should have come round the back looking for me, and not gone knocking on the front door. My mam'll have you here all week."

A great help he was. Still, we did manage to get out after a while and I had enjoyed looking at Mrs Metcalfe's pretty wedding photographs, all in white lace, not plain and dull like my mam's wedding at the beginning of the war.

We let ourselves out into Fred's backyard.

"You weren't to know," said Fred. "Kids always call round the backyards here. Call out the names, that's what we do. Then the mams don't keep you wittering on. You'll know for next time."

"I liked those baby photos though," I said, trying to get back at him a bit. "'Specially you with no clothes on."

"Get on with you," he said, blushing. "Hey Tom, shall I show you how to sledge ont' tip."

"Yeh."

"No," I said. "We're off to find the merman. You said yesterday. We've no time for sliding on tips."

"Ah we've plenty of time. He's not going anywhere. He's always there, either him or the cat." Fred was pulling a flattened cardboard box out from his backyard lavatory. "Away then Tom."

He was doing it on purpose, I could tell. The last thing I wanted to do was go sledging on a slagheap. I was worrying myself sick about what I'd said to Catterstyn. Then I thought about the cat and that gave me hope, but then I would remember tying Tom's braces round its neck and I would start feeling sick all over again.

Still, there wasn't anything I could do but wait for the boys. I certainly wasn't going by myself.

Tom was soon shooting down the gritty slope, screaming and yelling, fine grit flying into his face. I thought it looked terrible; you wouldn't catch me carrying on like that. I left them there and went round the front of the houses. I crossed the road and lent on the fence, looking over the valley to Fred's pigeon hut, remembering the story of the famine that Fred had told us up there. I'd asked Mam about it.

"Oh yes," she'd said. "Carlin Sunday. We've just missed it. Two weeks before Easter. We'll eat carlins next year, when it's Carlin Sunday. We used to skip to it when I was young – the Sundays in Lent.

Mid, Tid, Misere,

Carlin, Palm, Pace Egg Day.

Mind you, we had a rude rhyme too.

Carlin Sunday,

Wind on Monday,

Runs on Tuesday."

Then she'd laughed. My mam can be like that sometimes. Still I kept thinking about the famine ... everyone so hungry then... and why I seemed to keep waking up at night feeling hungry, too. It was almost as if the ghost of the hunger was coming to me through all those years, but why was it coming to me and no one else? I'd never heard of anything like that happening to anyone before.

"Hey!" Fred was shouting at me. "You have a go at this Jane ... come on."

"No fear," I said. "I want to be off to the cave."

"One go," he said. "You have one go, then I'll come."

There wasn't going to be any other way to get him to come, I could see that. He was stubborn, was Fred, so I agreed.

"Just one go. You've both to come after that."

I climbed the slithery slope, behind him. Tom egged me on from the bottom.

"Here now," said Fred, spreading out the battered cardboard. "It's sledging with no snow. Hold the sides up and dig in your heels to slow down. You'll like it, bet you will," and before I was settled he'd given me a great shove in the back and I was off, hurtling down with this great scream coming from my throat that I couldn't seem to stop. I dug my heels in like mad and rolled to the side as I reached the bottom of the slope. Best not let Mam see that, I thought. She'd go mad when she saw what it did to your shoes.

"I'nt it great ... i'nt it fine?" shouted Tom.

"It's not bad," I agreed, "but I'll not go again. You're to come now ... you know where."

At last they came along with me.

It was the cat that we saw, perched high up on a rock, gazing down the length of the valley towards the sea. He didn't seem to notice us coming, but looked past us, twitching his nose at the fresh salty air.

Suddenly Fred's idea of apologising seemed a bit foolish. It just looked like an ordinary cat ... a bit wild, but ordinary.

"You say it Fred," I begged, but he didn't look too keen.

Tom looked suspicious, I think it went through his mind that me and Fred were having a joke with him.

"Go on Fred," I said. "It's you who knows so much."

Then I realised that there was something strange about the cat. It was ignoring us on purpose. Any ordinary cat would have looked at us, we'd got so close, but this one still stared past us at the sea. I gave Fred a hard shove. He cleared his throat.

"Um ... er. We come to beg your pardon sir."

The cat turned two green eyes on him. It understood, there was no doubt of that.

Encouraged, Fred tried again. "I've come to ask pardon sir, for this ... er, young lady. She's only been in our village a short while. She didn't know it was so rude ... what she said."

Then both the cat and Fred looked at me. I wanted to turn and run, but to be fair, Fred had done his bit. Now it was up to me. I remembered that it had seemed to help before, so I stepped to the side and dropped my best curtsey again.

"I'm really sorry for asking what I did. I didn't know it was wrong. I've never met a ... anybody like you before. Please forgive me ... I didn't mean no harm."

The cat stared into my face. It never moved a whisker, but its eyes swam from green to blue, then suddenly it jumped down from the rock and headed for the cave. For a dreadful moment I thought it was offended again, but it stopped and looked back, as though to say 'come on', then it vanished near the rocks, close to the mouth of the cave.

We scrambled after it and when we reached the cave, there he was: Catterstyn, sitting on a rock, smiling at us.

Tom stood with his mouth hanging open. "Wow," he said.

I wondered how I could ever have thought him anything other than a merman. Now that I looked for it I could see that his skin had a green glow, with clear green tinges on his high cheekbones. His eyes changed from fierce leaf green to deep sea green ... swimming from one to the other, constantly changing. His hair and beard were silver and rippled like the fronds of a sea anemone.

Catterstyn chuckled, a sound like bubbling water.

"I should not have stirred myself to such a fury ... not at a poor land-child's words. I was all adrift."

He seemed kind enough now.

"Many tides have passed since I have spoken with mortals. I have grown prickly in my loneliness, but you can make a pretty speech, land-child, and I do forgive you."

That made me feel a lot better. My eyes went a bit watery and I had to blink hard, but Catterstyn had something to say to Fred.

"You are clever, fair youth. The tide would not catch you unawares. You knew me for myself."

Fred grinned and blushed. I could tell he was real proud to be called clever, but he wasn't so sure about the fair youth bit. The merman turned to our Tom, who'd been watching with eyes like saucers.

"Pleased I am to meet with you. I have that which is yours in my keeping."

We nearly burst with excitement when Catterstyn reached behind his rock and we saw a glittering fish's tail, gleaming from beneath the shining folds of his cloak. We kept quiet though; I think we thought it might be rude to point it out. The merman picked something up and held it out to Tom. It was his new yellow braces, all neatly rolled.

"Oh thank you sir. I didn't think I'd see them again. Me mam will be glad."

It made me feel ashamed to think we'd tied those braces round the neck of this ancient merman and tried to lead him like a dog. He seemed to read my thoughts though.

"Have no fear, dear land-girl. I knew you wished to help. Indeed I would have followed you, but whatever shape I take, I cannot leave the water's edge. And alas, there is another reason why I cannot leave this little beck."

His face clouded over with sadness. We couldn't think what to say. I remembered the cat sitting up on the rock, staring longingly down to the sea. "Have you always lived here?" Tom asked. The merman sighed. "Indeed I have not. I will tell you about myself if you wish to hear, though the telling will be long."

"Yes please," I said. "We'd really like that and we promise not to ask about that one thing."

We found ourselves a bit of rock to sit on. Our Tom grinned so wide it nearly split his face in two.

"I love a good story," he said.

CHAPTER FIVE

The Only Ones Who Know

"My memory fails. It ebbs and flows, but I will tell you all I can. I have so many tides to remember that I hardly know where to begin, but I should first tell you how I came to this cave; it was many tides ago."

And so he began. "When I was a young merman I took to adventuring, far from my home in the secret deeps. I thought it dangerous and exciting to see how close I might come to humankind, without them noticing. I loved to watch you mortals going about your strange lives and most of all I delighted in raising a storm, laughing at the havoc I caused."

I inched a little closer to our Tom ... I didn't feel too happy at the way things seemed to be going, but Catterstyn saw me.

"Nay," he said, "have no fear. I was young then, young and foolish. Now I have left such foolishness far behind me. I wish only well to humankind, and you will understand that soon.

"One time I swam along the coast nearby and saw the long sandy beach that stretches past the jetty. I had not seen so beautiful a beach for many a tide ... so peaceful, yet it had a wildness that called to me."

I knew just what he meant by that. I think that beach had called to me, too.

"I swam close in to rest in the shallows," he said. "I must have slept, for suddenly I opened my eyes and looked straight up into the face of a young girl-child. She examined me most carefully, her eyes bright with curiosity, her mouth parted in surprise, her nose sun-kissed, like yours, Jane."

Tom stared hard into my face. "Nah ... we call 'em freckles."

"You see," said Catterstyn, "'tis merfolk lore always to beware of humans, but the funny delighted look on that girl's face made me laugh. I flicked foam into her face, then swam away.

"Later that tide, a strange accident befell me. Indeed, it led to my lonely existence now. I swam near to where some fishermen worked a small boat. I am ashamed to say that it is a young merman's frolic to swim where men fish and chase the quarries from their nets. This time I was taken by surprise; there was no net in the water and the fishermen were pulling in a long line full of fish. A spare hook fastened itself in my tail. I thrashed around in the water trying to free myself and must have crashed into the side of the boat, for darkness closed in around me."

"Aye, they've always fished with long lines round here," said Fred. "But I'm sorry you were hurt ... was it bad?"

"It was a great hurt, but I found help where I least expected it. When I opened my eyes I found myself on shore, entangled in a net surrounded by the fisherfolk, their eyes full of dread. The men had thought me a great fish, and dragged me back behind the boat. Their fear, when they saw what they'd caught, showed in their muttering and their signs to ward off evil. A sickening pain in my shoulder told me that I was injured. I could neither move nor change my shape, so weak I was."

We stared silent at the merman. I could see how trapped he must have felt.

"Just at that moment," he said, "a moment I thought to be my last, the young girl that I'd seen near the beach came pushing through the crowd. She was the only one whose eyes held no dread. She knelt down beside me, gently touching my injured shoulder.

"She spoke to one of the men, who I later knew to be her father. She stood up angry and tearful, stamping her feet. Her father examined me with great reluctance, and at last he seemed to make up his mind. He directed his friends to pick me up. They carried me into a cottage close to the beach, but they turned their heads away, afraid to look me in the face, crossing themselves, and backing out of the small room that they'd left me in.

"The straw pallet meant for humans was agony to me, yet I was helpless, like a crab caught in a basket. The child was wonderfully quick; she brought wet seaweed to spread beneath me, and sea water for me to drink. She was busy and delighted that she'd got her way."

"It's a good job she did," said Tom. "Might they have killed you, do you think?"

"Nay, too much afraid for that," said Catterstyn, "but thrown me injured back into the sea I think, and I'd have surely died then, so badly hurt I was. My young friend took great care of me and her name I discovered was Enid. My wound gradually healed. and I began to regain my strength. Enid's father came each day to see me, watchful and anxious, but always kind. As the days passed, he and his friends became used to my appearance. They saw that I did them no harm and they began to show pleasure in my recovery. They brought fresh fish and watched marvelling as I ate it raw. Enid taught me to speak in the human's tongue and I learnt quickly, for I had nothing else to do, lying on my seaweed bed.

"The warmth of the sun waned and the leaf-shedding time began, and I longed to return to the sea, but Enid begged me to stay. I had grown very fond of her ... I'd shown to her alone my power of changing shape. The weeks flowed by and still I stayed, though my longing for the sea grew greater every day.

"One day I heard Enid's father talking to her. He told her that she was selfish keeping me there. He said that I was a wild creature and that I should be free."

"Poor Enid," I said. I could see why she'd have wanted him to stay.

Fred frowned at me. "Poor Catterstyn," he said. "Fancy being kept there by a selfish girl."

"Yes," I said, "but ..." It was no good. I couldn't explain it, but I knew I'd have wanted him to stay.

"I was very grateful to the old fisherman," said Catterstyn, "for I needed to return to the sea. I could never be really happy on land. Enid accepted what her father said, though she was miserable about it. I promised that I would return to visit her, and she followed me down to the water's edge. At last she forced a brave smile, and as I plunged gladly into the waves, she called out to me.

'Don't forget ... don't forget your promise.'

"My joy was so great at returning to the ocean that for a while I travelled happily wherever the sea carried me. At last I thought of Enid again, and realised with a shock that although only a short time had passed for me, three winters had passed for humans. Enid would be growing into a young woman; she would be thinking that I'd forgotten her.

"I returned as fast as I could, but as I swam along the shoreline, I saw very few fish and noticed a deadly silence from the tiny villages. Something was wrong. When I reached the little harbour a sense of dread fell on me. There was none of the calling and shouting, pushing out of boats and busy work that usually went on. I went further upstream until I could see the bridge. A small figure stood there gazing out to sea, an old woman I thought at first. She clutched a shawl tight round her shoulders, her back bent. As I came near she saw me and held out her arms to me. I saw that it was Enid. I could not believe the change in her. I had thought to find her a fine and bonny young girl ... like you, Jane."

I stared at Catterstyn. I think my mouth dropped open. A strange feeling of recognition had come to me. As soon as he'd begun to talk about his return, I'd known that he was to see the figure on the bridge ... the small figure in a long dress and shawl, looking like an old woman. I knew just what he meant, for I'd seen her, too. I wanted to tell Catterstyn, but Fred and Tom were both looking hard at me, waiting for me to speak. I couldn't think how to say it. I just shook my head.

"What was it? What was wrong?" I asked.

"Enid told me how one bit of ill fortune had followed another. The fishermen had found their catches very small and the fleet had sailed farther off, and not returned. At the same time there'd been a season of dry weather that eventually had given way to torrential rain, so that the meagre crops had been ruined. The countryside all around was affected and the people could find nothing to eat, neither from the land or sea."

"It was the famine," shouted Fred. "It must have been the famine."

"It was indeed, dreadful famine. The few animals people kept had died. The younger folk went searching for berries and roots, but the older ones had taken to their beds, too weak to get around. Enid was begging for help ... I was her only hope.

I comforted her as best I could, telling her that I would return the next day and bring food. I was touched to see her faith in me, for she returned to her cottage waving, sure that I could help."

"It was a good job you were there," said Tom. "You could save them ... couldn't you?"

"It was only through good fortune that I did," said Catterstyn. "I believe Enid thought that I could help in some sort of magical way. Alas I wished that I could. I could change my shape or raise a storm, but finding food was a different matter. I swam out to sea, desperately looking for fish. By darkness fall I had managed to catch four undersized herrings, hardly enough to feed Enid for one day ... then what of her family and friends? I thrashed about in the water, near out of my mind with despair.

"It was thick dark when I heard the creak and slap of a passing ship, three shoals' distance from the shore. It was just a small cargo boat but as I swam towards it my spirits rose. I could not tell what it carried, but I knew I must raise a storm more fierce than ever before. There was no other way to get the ship into the bay."

"How do you raise a storm?" asked Tom. "How can you make the wind blow strong?"

The merman smiled. "It is as easy for a merman as running and shouting is for a young lad like you.

It is what a merman does for enjoyment ... something that I held back and kept in check with the wisdom of old age. I lashed the sea to a great fury, stirring wild waves to hurl the vessel into the bay. I saw the sailors, stunned by the suddenness of the wind. They clung helpless to the masts. Wooden casks bobbed in the water and I let the waves subside and dived for a container. I broke it open ... to my horror I found it filled with tiny hard pebbles, like the clay marbles human children play with. I put a handful into my mouth and spat them out. This was not food. I had wrecked the ship for nought and brought into danger the sailors' lives. That thought made me act again. I guided the dazed men to the shore. Out from their cottages came the villagers, stumbling and weak. The only ones with strength to wade out were the young women and lads."

"Were the sailors all right then?" asked Fred.

"Yes, every one of them. I watched the villagers carry them into their houses to care for them ... I was desolate that I had failed them all.

"As the sun rose I fell exhausted against a rock. After I had rested I swam slowly into the bay, full of misery at the chaos I had caused. I saw the human folk paddling in the water. They pulled ashore the wooden casks and scooped from the water the little pebbles.

"I was surprised to hear the sound of laughter. I saw that everyone who could stand was down at the water's edge. Old folk paddled shakily in the shallows, bending carefully to gather. Small children carried baskets on their heads, splashing in the foam."

"I know," said Fred. "It's the carlins. We always knew about the carlins ... but we didn't know that the merman brought them."

"You have it right," said Catterstyn. "But it was all good fortune, for I didn't know what they were myself."

"Then it was you that started Carlin Sunday," said Tom. "It was you ... but we are the only ones who know it."

CHAPTER SIX

A Gentler Power

"I am weary," said Catterstyn, and I saw that his face had lost its fresh green look; it had turned grey and his hands trembled.

Fred looked worried. "Can we do anything to help sir?"

"Nay," said Catterstyn. "There is naught to be done. I've worn myself out with the telling and still I've not told you how I came to be living here. "

"That doesn't matter," said Fred. "We'd like to come again."

"Yes, that's it. Leave me to rest now. I have enjoyed your company. Please return soon and I shall be glad to tell you more, though I beg that you will not reveal my presence to other humankind."

"Oh no!" We all rushed to assure him about that. We got up to take our leave and thanked him. I could hardly bear to leave with the end of the tale untold, but I could see that he needed peace and quiet, so I followed the boys and we tiptoed quietly away.

"Well, I've such a surprise for you," said Mam. "You're going to be so pleased. I've just been up to the phone box to ring up Grandma and Grandad. They'd like you both to go over to Saltbum tomorrow and stay for a few days."

We both stared silent at her.

"You'll never guess what: they've bought themselves a television set; they've bought it just in time for the coronation. Won't that be grand?"

Again there was silence.

"I don't know what's got into you two. Don't you realise you'll be able to watch Children's Hour tomorrow? There's Muffin the Mule. It's what you've been wanting for so long."

I couldn't think what to say. There was nothing I could tell Mam that would make any sense. At last I said, "But ... but we've said we'll go out with Fred."

"Oh," said Mam. "Fred Metcalfe. I'm glad you've made a friend, but Fred will still be here when you get back. Go down to Fred's and explain to him. I've told your Gran you'll be delighted and I'll put you on the half-past-ten bus, and that can't be changed now."

I turned miserably to go, but Mam called me back. She was puzzled; well she would be.

"Jane, you said you didn't like it here? You said you hated it."

"Yes, well ... I'm beginning to like it now."

We got on the bus the following morning; there wasn't anything else we could do. We'd been down to explain to Fred and he'd understood how disappointed we were.

"Why don't you go down and tell Catterstyn what has happened?" said Tom.

"Ye…es. S'pose I could," said Fred.

I got the idea that Fred might feel just a bit scared going on his own and I was glad. It made me feel all cross to think of Fred getting to hear the end of the story and us not being there.

Grandad had retired from his job working in the Carlingrove steelworks just before the war, and they'd taken a cottage at Saltburn-by-the-Sea, a smart and pretty place, not far from Carlingrove. When I'd been a baby and we'd had a really bad time in Sheffield with the bombing. Mam had taken me and gone to stay with Grandma and Grandad, leaving poor dad in Sheffield to do his work in the blast furnace. Mam and me had stayed in Saltburn for a year or so, but towards the end of the war even Saltburn had come in for a few bombs, so Mam had decided to return to Sheffield and Dad, and it was after that that our Tom was born.

Tom and me had spent most of our summer holidays in Saltburn ever since. We loved it, going down to the beach every day. Grandma and Grandad rented a tiny chalet on the sea front, where they could make cups of tea and sandwiches. We kept buckets and spades in cupboards on the floor that had lids that turned into seats. There were Pierrot shows on the bottom promenade, Punch and Judy and a bandstand with a different band playing every afternoon. There were donkey rides and sandcastle competitions and fishing from the pier, and rides on the miniature railway up into the Italian gardens. If it hadn't been for us just getting to know Catterstyn, we'd have been thrilled to bits to spend a few days at Saltburn.

We did have a good time, even though I kept wondering what was going on back at Carlingrove. Grandma was excited about her television, and at last we saw all the programmes we'd heard so much about. Sometimes we even watched the morning programmes that were meant for testing the sets. It was the same programme each morning, and we got to know it rather well. Grandma's was a nine-inch set, with a screen of magnifying glass to make the picture bigger. It was like magic watching the pictures move, seeing little Muffin come clomping along the piano. Grandad said that one day there might be television sets with coloured pictures. I laughed at that. That would be too much like magic, I said.

We got spoilt and fussed over as usual by Grandma and that felt nice, and we stayed up late every night. It was just that all the time at the back of my mind I wondered about Catterstyn and his cave, and most of all about a lonely figure standing on a bridge: Enid, looking out to sea, hoping that help would come.

Mam came over to Saltbum and took us back to Carlingrove a few days later. We'd to start at the village school the following week and Mam said she'd need to get our things ready.

First thing on Wednesday morning we were off down to Fred's house and calling for him – round the back this time.

Fred had been down to see Catterstyn.

"I didn't stay long though," he said. "I told him you'd gone over to Saltbum and he said he'd keep his story till you came back."

I was glad of that, though I suppose it might have been a bit mean of me.

"He didn't seem all that well," said Fred.

"Well, he is old," I said.

"Yes ... but I don't think it's just that he's old," Fred said.

We went straight down the fields to see Catterstyn and I was so relieved to see him sitting there on his rock, smiling at us. There'd been a few times at Saltbum when I'd wondered if I'd dreamt it all. He looked fine to me; I couldn't think what Fred was worrying about.

"I'll tell you more of my story," he said, "but I can't seem to recall where we'd got to."

"You'd got the carlins," said Tom. "You'd wrecked the ship and the people were finding the carlins."

"Ah yes ... I remember now. At first I didn't understand what the carlins were. It was Enid who explained it to me. I found her gathering with the others and she greeted me with great joy.

"She waded out and flung her arms round me.

'This is your doing Catterstyn,' she said.

'But Enid... the people have gone mad with hunger," I said. "This is not food, you cannot eat these hard brown things."

"Enid laughed and shook her head. 'Oh Catterstyn, these are peas, parched peas. We call them carlins. We can boil them in water and they will be soft and good to eat. They are wonderful things to find for while they are hard they will keep and not go rotten. You have saved us, merman. I knew you would."

"Well, the villagers gathered the carlins from the sea until they had got them all. I stayed for a while and saw with amazement how the boiling water transformed them. I left the people happy and well. The fishing fleet had returned with a decent catch and they knew that they could begin planting for the next harvest."

"But that was not when you came to the cave?" said Fred.

"No, that was much later, many more tides passed before that time. Each spring at the time of the wrecking I returned to the village. I visited Enid and saw with pleasure how they'd taken up the custom of eating carlins and even named the place Carlingrove, to remind them of the cargo that had saved them."

"More tides passed and I saw Enid grow into a strong young woman. She married a fisherman, Jack Metcalfe, a dark-haired young man. Sometimes I think you have a look of him, Fred."

"And my name's Metcalfe," said Fred. "Do you mean that I could be a relation of your Enid?"

"I do not know, but Enid had six children and they all lived close by, but it is long, long ago, hundreds of years in your way of counting. I visited Enid every year of her life, until she grew old and died. To me her time seemed very brief. I missed her so, and I continued to visit Carlingrove, though I never became friends with another human, not after Enid."

"That's until now," said Tom. "We are your friends now ... we are, aren't we?"

Catterstyn laughed. "Indeed you are. You have banished my loneliness at last."

"But why is it that you stay here?" said Fred.

"Alas, I am trapped. Many times I visited this place and saw that all was well, then returned to the ocean, but the last time was different. I have always loved this running water and I came to spend a few pleasant tides beside this cave, but when I set out to return to the sea a strange laziness overcame me. With a great effort I struggled on downstream, but with each movement a great pain shot through me and a dreadful clanging and banging filled my head. There were many humans working near to the bridge, though they did not threaten me in any way ... too busy at their work to notice me, I think. At last I found myself unable to change my shape or even lift my little finger. The sky became filled with bright flashes like lightning ... I was very much afraid." We all sat very quiet and still. It was a frightening power that Catterstyn described, and yet a mystery.

"With a huge effort of will I dragged myself backwards upstream and took refuge in the cave. Slowly I regained my strength. Later I tried again to reach my sea, but the same thing happened. It was as though some power drained me of all my strength and each attempt I made took longer to recover from."

"Was there no other way you could go?" asked Fred.

"I cannot move far from the water's edge, even in my guise as a cat, but I decided to follow the stream inland, hoping that it might divide, so that I could find another way down. Alas, after two tides' journeying I found the source of the stream and there was no other way. I returned to my cave and resigned myself to making it my home."

"What can it be?" said Fred. "This thing that harms you?"

"I have thought about it many times, but I cannot find an answer. Some strange force or power ... invisible I think. Sometimes I feel it throughout the valley, but with a gentler power, that simply robs me of energy and exhausts me."

"Was that what stopped us, when we tried to take you away, when we thought you were just a cat?" I asked.

He nodded.

"You're tired now, aren't you Catterstyn?" said Tom, all worried.

The merman smiled. "Yes. I fear you must leave me to rest, though I beg you to return soon, for I value your company."

He was pale and looked worn out, so we quietly got up. I curtseyed and the boys both did funny stiff bows, then we set off back to the village.

CHAPTER SEVEN

Humans Are Strange Creatures

The next few days passed in a contented magic dream. Every moment that we could get away, we spent down at the merman's cave. He told us stories of strange sea creatures, monsters and adventurous merfolk, of far-away islands and beautiful caverns beneath the oceans.

Mam couldn't understand what had got into me, but she didn't worry too much, just smiled in a puzzled way to see me so happy, but the holidays were slipping away fast. On the last Sunday afternoon I'd been thinking about it all and worrying.

"All will be well Jane," Catterstyn had said. "The merman's good wishes flow with you."

The boys stared at me. I hadn't told anyone that I was worried about school, though I'd come to dread it. Again Catterstyn had known my thoughts. Then for a few dreamy moments strange jumbled pictures whirled through my mind: a girl standing on a bridge, looking out to sea; carlins falling through the sky, falling down from a warm cloud of grey feathers.

"Away home now Jane, we'll have to be going." Fred's voice cut through and I remembered school again. Catterstyn was smiling at me. I felt quite sure that he knew what I'd seen.

Monday arrived and I was sick at the thought of it all. We'd explained it to Catterstyn, and we'd planned to meet in the goats' field after school and go down to the cave.

School was as awful as I'd thought it could be. It was even worse than I'd thought, because of Fred. I knew I'd be in the same class and I even had some vague, silly idea that I'd sit next to him and he'd be kind and friendly and help me get used to it all. I should have known better.

"Now ... let me see, where should we put you?"

Miss Wetherall looked down the rows of desks. Fred sat at the back. There was an empty space beside him, but he stared out of the window.

Miss Wetherall looked severe, though not unkind, the sort that would be okay, so long as you didn't put a foot wrong. Every pair of eyes stared at me. That is, every pair of eyes but stupid Fred's. A fair-haired girl stuck her hand in the air.

"Miss. There's nobody next to me, Miss."

She didn't sound very keen, but she was nicer than anyone else. I went and sat down beside her, and stared at the lid of my desk.

Really we spent the whole day being told about the plans for the coronation. They went on about it all the time. When it was playtime I stood in the yard by myself. It was separate yards for girls and boys and another for the infants. I couldn't see Fred; I couldn't even go and say something nasty to him.

All the excitement that I'd felt about Catterstyn seemed to fade and I'd have given anything to have been back at my old school in Sheffield. They'd been planning a street party there, with all my old friends. They had funny ideas in Carlingrove ... there was to be a pageant done by my class, as we were the oldest, then a party in the school yard. I didn't think a party in a school yard would be much fun.

We went back into the classroom and did arithmetic. Fred didn't speak or even look my way. When the dinner bell rang, the girl who sat next to me said, "I s'pose you'd better sit with me."

After we'd eaten our dinner we went out into the yard again. I caught sight of our Tom, charging round the infants' yard, with a skipping-rope tied round another little lad's middle, playing horses, laughing and shouting. Trust him, I thought. He'll think it's wonderful.

"Can yer dance?" asked the fair-haired girl.

I stared at her. "Yes," I said. "I used to go to Constance Grant's."

"Oh?" she said. "I think I've heard of her. I go to Jean Hardie's. I do acrobatic." She bent backwards into a crab, then flipped her legs up into a perfect handstand. I was impressed. I felt better after that. She was called Sally, and although she was a bit of a show-off, she was all right. I showed her some of the ballet steps that I knew.

Back in the classroom we all heard about the coronation again. There was to be a pageant of St. George and the dragon. The teacher made all the boys stand up and walk to the front, then she picked out Fred and said he'd do. He was the tallest lad when he stood up straight. Fred was to be St. George. He went bright red and stared out of the window again. The teacher chose Sally to be the princess who was rescued from the dragon. Sally was delighted about that.

"I haven't decided how to do the dragon yet," said Miss Wetherall.

"I know how," I said.

There was silence and everyone turned to stare at me, so that I couldn't think why I'd opened my mouth.

"Yes?" said Miss Wetherall.

"Well ... at my other school we made a sort of dragon."

"Yes?"

"Well ... we made a paper maché head joined onto a long bit of green material and lots of people got under that, so that their legs looked like dragons legs and their heads made sort of lumps down the dragon's back."

There was silence again.

"Yes," said Sally. "That would work."

"Yes," said Miss Wetherall, nodding her head and smiling at me. "It could be as long as we like and no one need be left out. Yes – thank you, Jane, it's a good idea."

Suddenly everything seemed to change. A lot of the girls kept smiling at me and telling me their names and asking me where I lived. They seemed friendly after all, and I remembered then how Catterstyn had said that 'all would be well'.

I met Tom outside the infants' gates and we walked home together.

"It's good," he said. "I've lots of new friends. There's Colin and Ian, Graham and Kev."

"You haven't told them anything have you?" I asked.

"Told 'em. Course I haven't told 'em. I'd never give our merman away."

We had our tea and went straight out through the goats' field. Fred came running up behind us. "Wait ... give us a chance."

"Oh, you're speaking are you?" I spat it out at him. "Thanks for being so nice at school. Thanks for helping me out. Thanks for saving a place for me.

He frowned and looked amazed. "Save a place for you? Save a place for a lass? You must be daft."

I was still angry when we found Catterstyn, but somehow talking to him, with the water rippling past while I paddled my toes, was soothing. We told him about the pageant and the party and the coronation, though I think it was all a bit of a mystery to him.

"She will be Queen Elizabeth?"

"Yes, that's right," said Fred.

"All your queens are called Elizabeth?"

"Oh no, there was one ... our new queen will be Elizabeth the Second."

"Your queens live long?"

"Well Queen Victoria did, but I don't think they usually live any longer than ordinary folk."

Catterstyn shook his head. "Humans are strange creatures."

The weeks settled into a comfortable pattern. School was fine and we didn't have to do a lot of hard work, like arithmetic, as the preparations for the celebrations took over.

Each evening me and Tom met Fred in the goats' field and went to visit Catterstyn. One time he became very pale and poorly while we were there, so we left him to rest and returned the next day.

We asked if he felt better and he answered us a bit puzzled.

"I do not understand, my friends. As soon as you took your leave of me I recovered, but now I fear I swim down into sickness. I am sorry to say that it is affected by your presence. I cannot understand. It was not like this before."

We all took a step back, very upset.

"Do not look so sad," said Catterstyn. "Sit down where you are. Do not despair. We must fish this out. We must catch what is different. What is new?"

"What can it be?" asked Tom. "We are just the same."

"Is it all of us or just one of us that's making you ill?" asked Fred.

"How can we know?" I said. I had a nasty suspicion that it might be something to do with me, or those strange midnight hungers.

"You must all step close in turn," said Catterstyn.

I didn't like that idea at all. A horrid version of 'What time is it, Mr Wolf?', but you didn't know what would happen if you were caught.

Catterstyn smiled at me. He knew what I was thinking.

"Come Jane, step forward. It is most likely something that can be turned aright."

I gritted my teeth and stepped forward. I took another step, waiting for signs of strain. None came. Catterstyn chuckled, that humming bubbling sound.

"No, it is not you, Jane. Be at peace. Sit down again. Come Fred, your turn next."

Fred stood up looking miserable and moved carefully forward, but he went close to the merman without causing any distress.

"It isn't me – it can't be me," Tom shouted out, jumping forward.

Catterstyn's face drained of colour; he threw up his hands to protect himself. I grabbed our Tom and pulled him back, but I put my arm tight round him and kept it there. I knew how I'd have felt if it had been me.

Catterstyn drew a deep breath.

"Fear not, Tom," he said. "We will put this to rights. Let us consider. What is there about this young man that is different? Have you new apparel?"

Tom looked blank.

"Clothes," said Fred.

Tom looked down at his elbows. "Only new bits of darning."

We all looked at Tom and thought hard, but nothing came to mind.

Suddenly Tom started fishing around in his pocket.

"It's the only new thing I've got."

As he started to draw something out I realised what it was. He had badly wanted a mouth organ. He'd saved his pocket money up week after week and at last he'd been able to buy one in Saltburn. It was his best thing, he was really proud of it. It had a polished red plastic cover, with a gleaming steel reed that made the musical sounds, when you blew into it. He'd been driving us all mad at home, trying to learn to play 'God Save the Queen,' in time for the coronation.

As soon as he held it out, the merman groaned.

Tom shook himself free of my hands and backed away towards the stream, the mouth organ gripped tight in his fist. He turned and hurled the little instrument away, as far as he could, towards the sea.

"Oh Tom," Catterstyn said, getting his breath back. "Thank you, Tom, but I'm so sorry you have lost your new jewel."

I stared at Tom. I knew how much he'd treasured the thing.

"'S all right," he said. "As long as you feel better now. It's not a jewel, only a music thing."

Catterstyn looked puzzled but he seemed immediately better.

"Yes ... yes, I am quite recovered." His cheeks returned to their usual faint green glow.

I walked back along the path beside the beck with Tom. Fred was lagging behind and I kept glancing at our Tom, a bit concerned. He'd surprised me, throwing his treasure away like that.

"That were brave," I said. "Throwing away your new harmonica. A bit daft though – you could have just taken it home ... taken it away from the merman. Still it was brave."

"Don't care," he said.

"Hey up you two." Fred came charging up behind us. "I found it," he cried, waving the small instrument in his hand. "You don't want to lose a good little mouth organ like that."

Tom was delighted and reached for it. "I'll never bring it down here with me again," he said. "Thank you, Fred!"

"Well," said Fred. "It's set me wondering. Why should a little mouth organ bother him so much?"

We all walked on in silence, then Fred tried again.

"It could be the same thing that traps him here, couldn't it?"

"I don't know what you're on about," I said. I didn't want to know either.

"Don't you see? Whatever it is that traps him here, it makes him feel ill, just like the mouth organ did."

"It's just a bit of plastic ... and steel," I said.

"It makes a lovely sound though," said Tom, and he gave it a good blow.

Fred stood stock still, staring ahead of us. "That's it ... that's it." He pointed up at the overhead cable system. "Steel. Look at it. Those stands that carry the buckets are made of steel. If it's steel that harms him, the buckets and the cables make a bridge of steel right over the water and across the valley. The blowing part of the mouth organ is made of steel."

"You're right," said Tom. "I'm sure you are. Our merman's trapped by a bridge of steel."

"But this valley is full of steel," I said.

CHAPTER EIGHT

The Power of Steel

"Books," said Fred. "We need to find out about mermen and the best way would be to look it up in books."

"No," I said. "Mermen in books ... are from fairy tales, just stories. "

"You didn't believe there were such things as mermen, did you, but you've found out different now. If there are mermen, then what is said about them in fairy tales is probably true."

I didn't like the sound of this. I didn't see the point of it all.

"We'll have to go to the library," said Fred.

"Will they let us?" asked Tom.

"Course they won't," I said. "We haven't any tickets and they don't let children in without grown-ups."

"We could say we'd been sent by Miss Wetherall. We could say it was for our school work looking something up."

"Yes," said Tom. "I'll come with you Fred. Can we really find out what's wrong with Catterstyn?"

"Don't know," said Fred, "but we can at least try."

It was only an ordinary semi-detached house, but one of the biggest and oldest in the village. We pushed the door open and walked into the silent hallway, our feet making great clomping noises, disturbing the peace. The library part was upstairs.

I didn't like it at all. "We're going to get into trouble," I said. "And it won't do any good."

"You go home then," said Fred. "You go if you don't want to help."

He went marching up to this pretty young lady who sat at the desk. She smiled and looked surprised, as though she didn't believe a word, but she went over to a man who was filling shelves and whispered to him. They both turned and stared at us.

"They're wondering if we're hooligans," said Fred, and our Tom clapped his hand over his mouth to stop the giggles.

At last the man nodded. "No books to be taken out, though, and quiet in the library at all times," he said as he waved us in.

"Local history here," said Fred, whispering respectfully. "I'll look at that ... you see if you can find any folk-tales."

Tom followed Fred and I went over towards the window.

"Who does he think he is?" I muttered to myself. "Giving me orders. Telling me what to do."

The library had dim lights and felt stuffy; the mouldy smell of old books put me off. I glanced out of the window and noticed that you could see right down into the goats' field from there and to the old bridge beyond.

She was there ... the girl in the long skirt and the shawl, standing on the bridge staring out to sea. I rested my cheek on the window frame and turned to stare out to sea just like her. I stared and stared, watching for movement beyond the waves. Watched and hoped, while a grinding hunger and weakness gnawed in my belly.

Oh no, I thought. Not here. Not in daylight, not that awful feeling of hunger again.

I couldn't bear the dim, dusty library and gloomy shelves any longer. I ran out past the desk and clattered down the stairs. I crossed the road, screwing up my eyes in the sunlight and gulping in deep breaths of fresh air.

She had gone. The bridge was empty. I shook my head, puzzled. "Why?" I asked myself. "Why does she come and yet she never stays?"

Fred and Tom came out, both scowling at me. "Why did you do that? Are you going funny?" said Fred.

"I felt ill ... just didn't like it in there."

"It was hard enough getting in, without you acting daft."

"Yes," Tom added his bit. "They were nearly going to throw us out. I could tell."

"I couldn't help it. You wouldn't have found anything anyway."

"Well you're wrong, so there," said Tom. "Fred has found lots and he's written it all down." Fred pulled a mangled bit of envelope from his pocket, covered with his neat writing.

"Well?" I said. "What is so wonderful that you've found?"

"I've found that we were right."

"Right? How were we right?"

"It was in a book of folklore. It told you about mermen. Here it is: 'Mermen were thought to be salt-water spirits, with long hair and beards and fishlike tails. They were supposed to live to a great age.'"

"It's right, i'nt it?" shouted Tom, all excited.

"We knew all that when he told us," I said.

"No ... this is the bit. Listen to this. 'People who were afraid of mermen would carry iron with them, a knife or even a needle would do, for it had the effect of making a merman spellbound.'"

That did impress me I have to admit. "So that's what's wrong ... he's spellbound."

"Well, it says iron because they only knew how to make iron long ago, but now it could be steel as well. I think the steel could have greater effect ... it's strong stuff is steel."

"I didn't think it could be anything as ordinary as steel," I said. I wished I'd never said that.

"Ordinary! Steel's not ordinary," said Fred. "You'd better not let your dad hear you say that. My dad, he says that when they tap a furnace and white hot liquid steel pours out and floods into the moulds all glowing and turning golden ... he says it's magic, pure magic. I'm not surprised that it's steel. It's powerful stuff is steel and the buckets are full of iron ore, so there's iron there as well!."

Our Tom kept nodding his head at everything Fred said, backing him up all the time. You wouldn't think he was my brother.

"Oh well, " I said. "Perhaps steel is that strong, but I can't see why it should suddenly bother Catterstyn. The whole valley's full of steel and it's been there for ages."

"No it hasn't," said Fred. "Not ages. It's about a hundred years ago that they found the main iron seam and opened the steelworks. I know because we did it with Miss Wetherall. We learned all about it last term, before you came."

"A hundred years," repeated Tom.

"So what?" I said.

"Don't you see what happened?" said Fred. "It must have been then that the merman got trapped. He said that there were men working close to the bridge. They were building the overhead cable system and setting up the buckets, to carry the iron-ore up the hill. The steel stands stretch right across the river. Once they were there, they'd block his way down to the sea."

Tom was bursting with pride at the knowledge he'd gained: "Yes, our merman couldn't get down to the sea without going underneath the cables. He has to stay near the water, doesn't he?"

"There must be a way," said Fred. "Now we understand it better. There must be a way to get him back."

"We don't have to go mad about it," I said. "Catterstyn's all right."

"He's not all right," Fred snapped at me. "He longs for his ocean."

I couldn't share their excitement.

"He's not lonely," I said. "He's got us to look after him and keep him company. He's all right to stay here a bit longer."

The next time we visited Catterstyn we told him all about the book in the library and about the iron and steel. I don't think he understood it all. It seemed very strange to him that men went digging into the ground for special rocks that they could work at and turn into something as strong as steel.

"Magic indeed," he said.

"I wish we could think of a way to get you through," said Fred, but Catterstyn shook his head.

"Do not fret," he said. "I am happy that I have my visitors."

I pulled a face at Fred, to say 'told you so'.

The weeks went by and we still visited Catterstyn whenever we could. Plans for the coronation pageant took up a lot of our time. I have to admit that I got excited about it, such a wonderful day it was to be. The school was to be open all day, though we would be free to come and go as we liked. A big television set was to be hired for children and parents alike to watch the ceremony on. After the coronation service we were to parade around the village. Fred was to ride Hector, the big horse that pulled the greengrocer's cart. He'd to wear a cardboard helmet painted silver and chain mail knitted from dishcloth cotton, which was also painted silver. Over that he was to wear a white tunic with a red cross stitched to the front.

"Fred's a fine looking lad right enough," said Mam, when I told her about it. "He'll look smashing up on that horse. Don't you wish it was you going to be the princess?"

"No," I said, pulling a face. "I'm to be the dragon's head because it was my idea. Dragon's head is by far the best thing to be."

After we'd paraded round the village we were to have a pretend fight outside the school, then we were to go and have a big feast at long tables in the playground, and be presented with special mugs with a picture of the crowned Queen, as she would be then.

Fred seemed to be very quiet, and I wondered if he was scared about riding Hector on Coronation Day. He was a really big horse, but he was good-tempered. We all saved sugar lumps to give him when he came round the houses with old Wilf, selling greens from door to door.

It was the evening before Coronation Day that I found out it was something very different that was bothering Fred. We were walking back from the merman's cave, and I felt really excited and happy. They'd even put bunting on the overhead cable system and the whole village looked a real picture, but Fred walked ahead of us, with his hands thrust deep into his pockets and his shoulders all hunched. He kept stopping and looking as though he wanted to say something, but then went on again without managing to spit it out.

"It's that Hector i'nt it?" I said. "You'll not fall off ... he's far too steady. You've no need to worry about that."

Fred narrowed his eyes. "Nah," he said. "Hector's all right. It's Catterstyn ... that's what's on my mind. We've got to do something about it. We've just got to try."

"Oh," I said. "Well there's nowt we can do, so just shut up."

"We could try something," Fred insisted. "We haven't even tried."

"What could we try?" said Tom. "I'll try it, if you can think of something Fred."

"You would," I said. "Jump off a cliff you would, if Fred said."

"Look," said Fred. "If Catterstyn turned himself into the cat, then perhaps we could carry him down under the steel girders. The steel doesn't hurt us, it's only him."

"Oh no," I said. "Don't you remember what happened when we tried to take the cat before? He turned as heavy as lead. I know, it was me that held him, not you."

"I'd try," said Tom. "I'd try it Fred."

"We didn't understand it then," said Fred. "We could all help with the carrying and we might manage to get him through."

"It wouldn't work," I said. "And even if it did, what would he do but swim away and we'd never see him again."

Fred glared at me. "That's it," he said, and his face flushed all red. "That's the reason you won't help. You want to keep him there like a caged animal. You're just like that other girl he used to know. You're a selfish pig."

I was furious and tears burst from my eyes. "We'd never see him again. He's so old."

"That's why we've got to try. He's dying, you know. He's going to die, trapped in that cave, stuck there by that little stream when he should be in the ocean. Those rocks up there, they're full of iron. The whole valley is full of iron; they're draining his strength and making him ill. I don't know how you can be so mean. Well, you needn't help. I'm going to try without you. I'll do it on me own."

"I'll help you Fred," said Tom. "I'll do anything you say. I'll do anything to make our merman happy."

"You're both horrid," I yelled. "You've spoilt it. I hate you both. You've spoilt it all for me."

I ran out of the field and over the road, up the stairs into my bedroom, and howled and howled until I was tired out.

I woke up in the dark. I couldn't think what had happened at first, but then I remembered that Mam had brought me some supper, looking all worried, but the tray was still there and I hadn't eaten anything. I couldn't forget the row I'd had with Fred and I felt sick and miserable. I walked to the window and looked out into pitch black dark. I couldn't work it out. I could usually see the dim lights of the steelworks and the dark creaking shapes of the buckets, swinging on their cables. There was nothing now ... just deep darkness, and hunger in my belly.

I crept downstairs and quietly opened the front door. I couldn't find the gate in this heavy darkness, but I seemed to be standing in the road, though it was soft beneath my bare feet. I could find no fence, even though I put my hand out for it, and there were no steel stands or buckets swinging above my head.

Then I saw her, down on the bridge, the one I'd seen before. A gentle light came, not from the dawn, but from her ... Enid. She turned towards me, slowly raising her hands ... pleading.

"Yes," I said. I whispered it, but she heard. She understood. She knew how hard it was, she'd found it difficult too, but it had to be done. The merman must return to the sea.

CHAPTER NINE

A Cloud of Love and Hope

I put my head down into my hands and cried. It wasn't misery; it was a kind of relief. I'd made a decision and it had been a hard one, but I knew that it was right. I knew when it had to be done too ... and it would be perfect timing.

I calmed down and lifted my head. Enid had gone and the dawn light was creeping over the hilltop. The buckets were back, creaking and groaning above my head. But the hunger was still there. I laughed out loud, realising that it was true hunger. I hadn't eaten since yesterday dinnertime. I quietly went back inside and ate the dry sandwiches that Mam had carried up for me.

I couldn't get to sleep again, for my mind was full of ideas. I woke Tom as early as I dared. He looked surprised.

"Don't make a sound. Get dressed! We're taking the merman back to the sea."

A great grin split his face and he jumped out of bed.

We walked down to Fred's through the back alleys, all hung with flags and bunting.

"What are we going to do?" Tom asked. "How are we going to do it?"

"Tell you when we get to Fred's."

I threw some pebbles up at Fred's bedroom window. They made a tapping sound, but there was no sign of Fred. Only Mary came and made faces at us.

"There," said Tom, pointing behind me. "He's coming down the backs."

It was Fred and his dad.

"Now then," said Mr Metcalfe. "There's more early birds here."

"Where've you been?" asked Tom.

"Putting pigeons on the train for York," said Fred. "They're going to let them fly, when she leaves for the palace. Our Bluey'll be first back."

"Aye, there'll be pigeons flying all ways, to celebrate the day," said Fred's dad. "But I'm away inside for my breakfast now."

Fred stared at me; I could tell that he was still angry. I think he wondered whether to follow his dad and ignore me.

"You were right," I said.

He stared even harder and up went his eyebrows.

"You were right. We should try to take the merman back to the sea. I knew that ... I just couldn't bear to think of him going."

Fred smiled, but he never said a word; he was good like that.

"If we're going to do it though, we should do it today."

"What?"

"Yes, today. If we carry him down, like you said ... well, we need it quiet ... no one around. We don't know what might happen. We don't want anyone interfering."

Fred nodded slowly. "You mean while the coronation is going on."

"Yes. They'll all be listening to their wireless sets or watching their televisions."

"What about your pageant?" said Tom.

"We'll have to be back for that of course."

"Like you said, we don't know what will happen ... we might not get back in time."

"We've all morning to get it done and it's the best chance we'll ever have," I insisted.

"Aye," said Fred. "I think you're right. The village'll be deserted. But you'll miss it all. I wouldn't have thought you'd do that."

"It doesn't matter. It's him that matters, Catterstyn ... though we haven't asked him yet, have we?"

"He won't say no," said Fred.

"No, he won't say no," said Tom.

We set off down through the goats' field, all wearing our best new clothes. We'd have been better in our old things and wellies, but it couldn't be helped. Our mams had been saving since Christmas, and I loved the new black patent leather shoes and blue-flowered cotton dress and white cardigan. I'd a new blue ribbon in my hair and I felt really smart. Fred and Tom both had new grey flannel shorts and new knitted Fair Isle pullovers over fresh white shirts.

"Did your mam think owt was up?" said Fred.

"No. She's off to Saltbum with Dad to see it all on Grandma's television, though they're coming back for the pageant and the party. All Mam's worried about is whether the Queen will faint or not ... her being so young and the crown being so heavy."

We found Catterstyn sitting on the rock in front of his cave. He was pleased to see us and admired our new clothes. He was very surprised when we told him what we planned to do and he wouldn't agree, not at first.

"There is nothing I want more than to return to my sea. But I cannot let you take such a risk, my dear friends. There may be great peril in such an undertaking ... I cannot know. I do not understand this steel and its power. It is strange human magic, that your fathers create."

He wanted to go, we knew that, but he thought that something nasty might happen and he was afraid for us. I don't think he cared about himself.

"This is your special day," he said. "See, you are dressed in lovely apparel. Let us think about this adventure another time."

Then we all talked at once and tried to explain that there would never be another chance as good. It was our Tom who managed to say the right thing in the end.

"Look Catterstyn," he said. "We are your friends now, right? We know how much you love your sea, and we can't be happy till we've tried to take you back."

Catterstyn sat in silence, his face sad and thoughtful. We stood quiet then, waiting.

"Such friends," he said, at last. "I never thought to find such brave and gentle folk amongst the humankind. Never since Enid have I had such noble friends ... such understanding."

Then suddenly he was gone and the cat was there in his place, blinking at us and stretching its back. We knew that he had consented. We would try to make our plan work.

As we set off towards the steel stands, it started to rain. Not a heavy rain, just a miserable drizzle that wasn't good for our clothes, but it seemed to mean good luck for Catterstyn, as water of any kind gave him strength.

We walked along the path, keeping close to the beck. Catterstyn in the guise of the cat paddled down through the water as far as he could. He went well at first but as the steel cable stands came into sight we could see that he slowed down. He carried on, determined to get as far as he could, but each step was an effort. I couldn't bear it, so I balanced on the stones and picked him up from the water.

"Phew," I said. "He weighs a ton already."

"Give him here," said Fred. "You'll soak your dress."

"No ... I'm all right. You save your strength for later."

I went on, but with each step he became heavier and I had to ask for help. Eventually all three of us were carrying him. The cat gave a sad mew and closed his eyes. It was all the more difficult because though he was so heavy, he was small, and we had to go all bunched up together, treading on each other's feet and Fred walking backwards.

The closer we got to the cables the harder it became, but we got quite close. Then we had to stop; we couldn't move at all.

"I can't hold him," Tom cried. "He's going to slip. I'm dropping him."

I was scared, for he'd grown so heavy that it was hard to set him down gently.

"Nay," said Fred. "Bend your legs, one at a time. Let him go steady."

I copied Fred, my heart pounding and my forehead wet with sweat. Our Tom was upset.

"I can't do it," he said. "I can't hold him up." His face crumpled; he was trying hard not to cry.

"We'll rest a bit," said Fred, "then try."

I nodded, but I couldn't see how we'd manage to get going again, and all the time the water cat lay on his side, his eyes closed, his breath coming harsh and fast. Fred kept staring up into the sky, narrowing his eyes.

"Bluey," he shouted, "my Bluey!"

"Can't be," I said. "Can't have flown from York already."

"No," he agreed, puzzled. "But my Bluey it is."

Sure enough the pigeon came fluttering down through the rain and perched on Fred's head, rubbing her beak against his cheek, then suddenly up she went, back into the sky, swooping round in a big circle above our heads. She didn't fly away, but carried on circling round and round. Then I saw that it wasn't only Bluey. There were two birds, then three, then another and another ... till all the pigeons of Carlingrove filled the sky. We stared up at them. I couldn't believe it ... I'd never seen such a thing. Then down swooped Bluey, touching the tip of Fred's ear, and up she went, landing on the steel stand. Down went the others, following the path of her flight, so that we all ducked our heads and fine grey feathers floated in the air. The nearest steel stand was covered with twitching slate-coloured bodies.

Fred's mouth dropped open. "They know ... they know and they want to help."

He was right, there was no doubt of that. Each pigeon drooped its wings, spreading them wide to the tips. A living curtain of shimmering feathers, protection from the power of steel.

"Ain't they grand," said Tom, laughing now. "They're really grand."

I picked up the cat. "It's working," I shouted.

The cat was still heavy, but we could move him again. We all lifted together and step by step we began to pass beneath the bridge of steel.

We had to put our heads down and push forward, for the rain fell heavily now, slapping sharp and stinging into our faces, driving us back, and a terrible wind whirled around the stands, whipping back the hair from our heads, cutting the breath from our throats so that we gasped. Then gradually a clanging sound began, faint at first, but growing loud, filling the space between the stands. It grew to a deafening roar, and a hammering, like the sounds of the forging that had given the stands their birth.

We struggled on. There was no going back. I feared from his limp body and bedraggled fur that we'd harmed our water cat, bringing him this far. But we couldn't make things worse ... we had to go on. The noise grew so that it clashed and clammered inside my head. I wanted to drop the cat and cover my ears, but I dug my fingers even harder into the drenched fur, gritting my teeth and grinding them together, anything to stop myself from letting go. Blinding flashes like blue lightning exploded in our eyes, so that we could not see clear and stumbled and trod on each other, unsure of which direction we took. But despite it all I somehow knew that the pigeons still went with us, fluttering and perching where they could, a determined cloud of love and hope, moving above us.

Though we heaved and pushed with all our might, we stuck fast, right in the middle, and though the pigeons gathered around us, their gentle feathers were not enough to protect us from the full force of the magical power of steel.

Tom's face, pressed into the cat's side, frightened me. His ashen cheeks were dragged hollow with pressure, and rain and sweat poured down his face, his curly hair lashed straight and flat against his head.

We never should have done it, I thought. What have I done to our Tom? I knew I must look the same and, though I tried, I couldn't turn my head towards Fred. The wind-torn body of the cat burst into violent trembling that almost jolted him from our arms. He raised his head to the remorseless power that beat us back and he gave one long, low, thrumming howl of despair, which echoed with heart-breaking loneliness between the stands and was thrown back at us with scorn.

Catterstyn's head dropped.

He's dead, I thought. We've killed him. We've killed our merman and we are trapped, stuck forever in this pitiless prison of steel. I couldn't believe it. Even the birds had given their help. How could we fail so miserably when Enid had shown me what to do? As I thought of Enid, the hunger came with her.

Not now, I thought. Not now. I can't bear it.

Then suddenly my mind was racing. I'd been stupid and slow. Enid had come to me last night and when she came, the steel stands had vanished. If she came now, they might go again. I must make her come to help us.

I screamed, though no sound came. Screamed inside my head. "Enid ... Enid ... he's your merman too."

Then waves of hunger came washing through and I was glad. She'd heard ... she was coming. I looked up at the bridge.

Gently a shadow formed, steadily growing solid, till I saw her clear and close for the first time. So clear that I could see her worn plaid shawl, her rough woven dress all mended and darned, her thin scarred hands, but what drew me was her face. A face I knew ... the face in my mirror and yet not, for it was thin and white, with purple shadows beneath the eyes ... but still it was my face. So clear and strong she became that she was the only reality. The cables and stands and the works beyond them faded, hazy and flickering, and the pigeons soared up into the sky. The noise ceased, the wind dropped, and I let go of the cat and fell backwards, stunned and shocked by the frightening power of silence. Then gradually I noticed a gentle, trickling sound ... the only sound in the valley ... the beck gurgling past us. Suddenly with a whoosh and a flurry of feathers the pigeons flew overhead and went, arrow-straight out to sea.

I was free. Free to move and speak and understand. Tom and Fred were huddled together, crouched on the ground, still clinging to the cat.

"Now," I shouted. "Now ... it's gone."

Fred stared. "What?"

"The sea ... give him here. He needs the sea."

I picked the cat out of their arms and turned towards the beach. I hurried along a strange cobbled path, following the flight of the pigeons. I hugged the poor lifeless body to my chest, then with a greater sense of urgency I started to run. There was no time to look for Enid on the bridge. I ran through a quiet landscape that was not Carlingrove and yet was somehow familiar. There were a few thatched cottages and fishing boats pulled up on the shingle, but the pigeons were my guide and I followed them, running as fast as I knew how, and soon I was stumbling and slipping over the rocks, and out onto the lovely sands, the sands that I knew ... Cattersty beach. I went straight into the sea.

Fred and Tom came panting up behind me. They bent down, watching, all worried, as the water soaked into the dull fur.

"I saw a whisker twitch."

"No."

"Yes ... yes it did."

A whisker twitched again and the cat wriggled its nose, snuffling at the salty air. He opened his eyes and I let him go. Catterstyn sprang into life, diving headfirst into the waves. In an instant the cat was gone and a silver fish's tail swished through the water. The merman's head rose. I've never seen a face so full of joy; I'll never forget it. Just then I was glad that we wore our best clothes, dripping and crumpled though they were. The church bell at Carlingrove started ringing a cheerful ding, ding, ding; then the old church at Saltbum could be heard faintly ringing out its peal, too. Somewhere at the back of my mind I knew that Queen Elizabeth was crowned and leaving the Abbey in her golden coach, but it felt as though the bells rang out for our merman, who swam in his ocean again.

The rain stopped and the sun sent a rainbow shooting across to the horizon.

We stood and watched as he dived, then came up in a fountain of foam. We watched silent, with the pigeons circling above us, watched as we saw him change. The silver hair swung with life, flinging green and golden lights into the sky. His eyes swam dark and keen, and his laugh — no longer bubbling, but the sound of crashing breakers – burst upon our ears. He went fast and true, far out to sea, then back to us. A creature in its full strength, brimming with energy and life.

Tom's fingers tightened on my arm. "Our merman," he said. "Our merman isn't old at all."

CHAPTER TEN

Enid's Gift

Catterstyn swam far out towards the horizon and we thought we'd seen the last of him, but then he came back, laughing and waving to us.

"Come here, my friends, come into my element."

We all looked at each other, surprised, but then without needing to agree we waded in, up to our knees. Catterstyn met us in the shallows.

"My dearest friends," he said. "I can never repay you, but there is one thing I can do. It is the only gift I have to give. I wish to share with you the secret of my age."

I caught my breath, remembering how I'd upset him when we'd first found him, down by the beck.

He nodded. As ever, he'd known my thoughts.

"Strange it must seem to you, my dear land-child. It is a secret that must never be begged, but if the trust is great enough, then it can be freely given. It will put me in your power ... if you call, I will come. I know that you will never abuse my gift, but if your need is great, then do not hesitate to call. That is the gift I have to give."

We stood there, the waves lapping round our clothes ... still and silent. We listened carefully as he entrusted to us his great secret, then he headed for the deep water, and we knew that he had really gone.

We watched, long after he'd disappeared, and it was only when the pigeons turned from the sea and flew off towards the lofts that we walked back out onto the beach. I couldn't see for the tears that welled up in my eyes, and I was grateful to catch the movement as Fred quietly wiped his cheeks. Tom just let his tears flow, though he smiled through them, and I knew just how he felt.

"We've done it," he said, and we all broke out into wonderful laughter that filled us with relief.

Then I remembered Enid, and wondered about her.

"Did you see somebody, standing on the bridge?"

"No," said Fred. "Anyone would have thought we were mad."

"But didn't you see the girl ... wrapped in a shawl?"

Fred was truly surprised. "No. Why are you asking?"

"Oh … it's nothing ... just that I thought I did."

I was puzzled. Was it really only me that had seen her? I tried again.

"Didn't you see anyone? She was there when the buckets vanished."

Tom laughed at that. "How could the buckets vanish?"

"But how do you think we got through?"

Fred stared at me. "You did shout something out, as though you thought they'd gone, but they were still there. You just got real upset I think. It's no good asking me how we got through. How did the pigeons get here? How did they know what to do? Where did that horrible noise come from? None of it makes sense ... I'm just so glad we did it."

"Yes," said Tom. "We did it and it was grand."

I opened my mouth to say more, but I didn't know where to start, how to explain about Enid ... and suddenly I wasn't sure I wanted to. Perhaps it was right that Enid just came for me. If that was true, it was so special perhaps it wasn't for sharing.

"Hey, we've forgotten the pageant!" said Fred.

"Run! Run back," said Tom. "You might be just in time."

We tore back, over the rocks and up past the jetty, though I looked carefully at the old bridge. It was full of little kids in fancy dress, waving flags and waiting for the pageant to begin.

We did reach the school, just in time. Everyone else was dressed up and Sally, all fine in her silver dress, with a tall hat and floating veil, was looking rather crossly down the road for her St. George.

Then it all happened so fast that I can't remember it clearly. I managed to hang up my wet frock in the classroom, before Mam saw it. I struggled quickly into my green tights and blouse and climbed into the dragon's head. Then off we went, and we'd practised it all so many times that I didn't have to think carefully what to do. It was fun and I had this glad sort of feeling all the time, and Fred did look grand in his cardboard armour. We had our pretend fight; I enjoyed it so much that it was only when I saw through the dragon's gaping mouth that Fred was looking annoyed I realised he'd stabbed me three times, and the dragon really ought to die. The dying was dramatic and went on for quite a while.

When I saw Sally climb up onto Hector and ride away with Fred, just for a moment I wished it was me ... but then I made the dragon jump up and bow and everyone clapped and cheered, and I knew that being the dragon was best.

We kept our pageant clothes on for the party, and Mam was there with Grandma, both handing round the cakes. Everyone was excited; they talked and laughed and went on about the queen's dress and her cloak; the weight of the orb and sceptre, not to speak of the crown; and the wonderful golden coach with the famous figures painted on the sides. What grand news it was about the two brave men who'd climbed the highest mountain, and how it was the start of a fine, new, exciting time. Tom took out his mouth organ and played 'God Save the Queen,' quite perfectly. Everyone clapped and sang along as he played, but all I could think about was Catterstyn's joyful face, as he swam through his sea again.

There was jelly and ice-cream, chocolate buns, cream horns, eclairs, iced biscuits and fizzy lemonade. When we'd all stuffed ourselves with food we were presented with a coronation mug full of wrapped chocolates. It had a picture of the Queen's head on the side and lots of different flags. We got a book of pictures of the royal family, too.

The sun shone, the works' band played and there was dancing till late at night. Mam let us stay up, though I must have been tired for I can't remember how I got to bed.

I just know that I woke up and knew that I was in my bedroom and it was dark. A wind was blowing and rain was pattering against my window and I was hungry.

For a moment I thought I'd dreamt the whole thing of taking our merman back to the sea but then I could remember it all so vividly I knew it had really happened. I was puzzled because I thought we'd done all we could, but I pushed back the bedclothes and got up: there was no mistaking it ... Enid wanted me.

I let myself out of the front door as quietly as I could, but the wind caught it and slammed it smartly shut behind me. I crossed the road and looked down towards the bridge. There was no small figure that I could see and the buckets on their cables creaked above me. The wind was chilling and the rain was steady, but the hunger was still there, and I set off down the field, careless of my bare feet and trailing cotton nightie.

I kept looking at the bridge, but I couldn't see her there. When I reached the edge of the bridge I stopped, knowing suddenly that something *was* going to happen.

A flickering shape grew from the darkness. She was closer to me than ever before, though her outline was faint, shimmering dimly. I did not turn my head to check, but I knew that the steel stands were still there, behind me. Slowly Enid raised her hand. I couldn't think what it was that she wanted ... some kind of greeting it seemed, needing some response. Then all at once I understood. I raised my own hand in reply and I thought I heard a gentle voice speak one word, "Farewell."

Then she faded and with her went the hunger. I felt alone and quite certain that Enid would not come back again.

I stood very still; I don't know how long it was, but suddenly I realised that I was standing on a bridge in the middle of the night, soaking wet and cold, in my nightie. I pulled myself together and turned to go when I heard a faint sound.

I stopped and listened. I heard it again: a tiny cry. It came from the bridge. I went carefully towards it, straining my ears to pick up the noise.

I went into the middle of the bridge, peering into the shadows, then I stopped. There was no need to hunt around. I went straight to the spot, the place where Enid had appeared. I stretched out my hand, down towards a patch of shadow, darker than the rest. I knew what I would find; my fingers touched wet fur.

My hand closed around a tiny shivering body. I stood up, holding a trembling kitten to my face. This was no ghost, this was a live creature. I could smell wet fur and feel the minute heart pounding frantically. A creature in distress. It needed food and warmth. As I turned from the bridge, a surprisingly loud, rumbling, purring reached my ears. A warm blanket of happiness spread from the kitten to me. Enid had left a gift.

I struggled up through the wet grass at the bottom of the goats' field, hugging the kitten tightly to my chest. Two lights were moving up the road at the top and a torch was turned in my direction. There was a swishing of grass and the light of the torch bobbed down the hill towards me. I froze, but Fred's voice called out my name.

"I knew you'd be down here," he said. "Though what you're up to I don't know."

"Fred ... I'm cold."

"I should think you are. What you doing? You've got half the village out looking for you." His warm hand found my freezing shoulder. "Now then, you are cold. You must get back quick or you'll catch a chill." His voice sounded anxious and in a moment his thick donkey jacket was thrown round my shoulders and his arm went round me. Half pushing, half carrying me, he got us to the top of the hill.

"Fred, you'll never believe it. I found it all soaked."

"Dreaming, that's what you been doing. Dreaming about Catterstyn. It's no wonder after what happened."

"No. It's real. A kitten, all wet."

"Your mam and dad are that worried. Your mam's been down to our house looking for you."

I heard my dad's voice calling from the road.

"That you lad? Have you got her? Ah, that's grand. Tell our Ivy. Metcalfe's lad's found her. "

Dad picked me up and carried me into our kitchen. It was all very surprising; the room was full of people and Fred's mam was stoking the fire. Dad sat me in the chair beside the hearth and Mam burst into tears.

"Now then Ivy," said Fred's mam, hugging her. "She's found. She's wet and cold, but there's no harm done."

Mam mopped her eyes and looked angry at me. "I don't know what you think you're doing. You've had me scared to death, and all our neighbours up looking for you."

Dad laughed. "That's it, tell her off, get back to normal."

"It's the excitement of the day," said Fred's mam. "It can make them very unsettled ... sleep walking, that's what it is."

"Yes, I don't know what else they've been up to today," my mam said. "Her new dress was soaked and our Tom's ruined his best shoes."

All I could think to say was, "I'm sorry Mam, but I've found a kitten. I'm sorry Mam." I pushed back Fred's jacket and held up the little cat. It was the first time I'd been able to see it properly. Two bright eyes looked steadily into mine. Damp grey fur was fluffing at the edges. Loud purring began and the front paws pounded up and down on my arm, prickling my skin, making me giggle.

"Oh Mam," I said. "You'll let me keep it, won't you? I found it down on the bridge."

"Food," said Tom, climbing onto the dresser in his pyjamas. "It needs food ... we had tuna-fish for our sandwiches."

"Ah, there's many a kitten been taken out from the towns to be dumped over that bridge," said Fred's mam. "I reckon this is a right lucky one."

"Please Mam. I've rescued it, you see."

"Eeh dear. I suppose it can stay," said Mam, shaking her head.

Fred knelt down beside me and tickled the fragile furry head.

"Look at its fur," he said. "You're going to get this one dry."

Author's Note

Theresa Tomlinson lives in Whitby with her husband and cat Jezza!

The Water Cat was inspired by my early childhood memories of living in Carlin How in a house that was next to the steel works gates. I was always fascinated by the legend of the Skinningrove Merman and linked it together with the custom of eating carlin peas on Carlin Sunday, along with one of the possible explanations behind the tradition.

My dad was the vicar of Carlin How and Skinningrove – I turned the two villages into one for my story and enjoyed reviving the happy memories that I have of living in that area.

The story was first published in 1988, but had been out of print for many years – feeling sad about that, I decided to bring this slightly updated version back into print once again, with the help of York Publishing Services – and the design work of my clever daughter Rosie Maddocks.

Theresa Tomlinson – September 2024

Website – theresatomlinson.com